MAYE CLARK

The Caged Bird

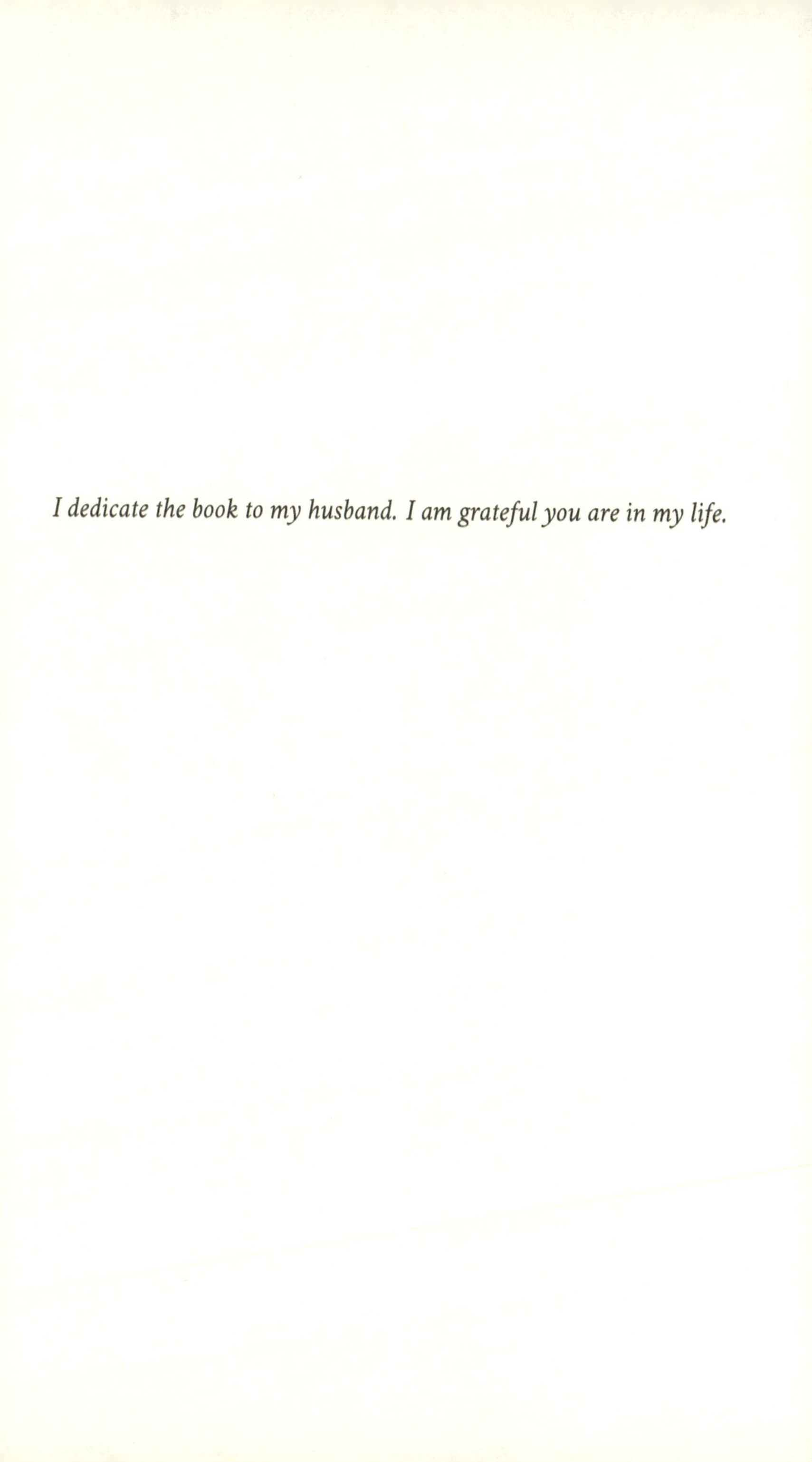

I dedicate the book to my husband. I am grateful you are in my life.

I am a bird.
I want to fly.
But I can't.
I wither from anxiety.
I whimper from depression.
I am misunderstood why I ruffle my
feathers.
I'm still in a cage full of misconcep-
tions.
I try to be free but—
It scares me
And I'm left—
In the dark
I put myself in the cage—
Hiding from the world
I am a bird

MAYE CLARK

Contents

Acknowledgement

I would like to thank my husband for supporting me. He has been the rock for me to hold on to. I would like to thank my therapist for helping me deal with this trauma and be able to move forward with strength. I am grateful for my parents and the love and support they have always given me

BEFORE

CHAPTER 1: THE LAST CHILD

I was always last in everything, and this began when I was born the last of five children. My mom told me my sister prayed for a girl so that she could have a sister. After having three crazy brothers, it makes sense my sister wanted another girl to balance out the craziness. I balanced out my family when I was born, and I still find myself calm in the storm. I was born in a loving home. Well, it looked like a loving home on the surface.

My mom told me that she had a miscarriage before she had me, and it makes me wonder what life would be like with another sibling. Would my parents stop having kids after my sibling that never was or would I still be the last of six kids? This led to an interesting beginning of life, and I heard different versions of my birth. One said I pooped in utero, and another said that I had the cord wrapped around my neck but nonetheless, my heart still stopped, and my mother still had to do an emergency C-section when I was born. I was a miracle and my family fawned over me as a baby.

I don't remember that part of my life till probably when I was three years old. Those years seemed innocent enough. I played and practically lived at my best friend's house next door. We would do childlike activities but there was something looming over my house. It was something I did not understand, and it left my siblings with trauma to this day. My mother is mentally ill and ended up in an institution for six months. She was depressed but as a bubbling three-year-old, I did not notice. Her depression turned into a lifetime struggle that she still deals with to this day.

The most prominent memory of my childhood was when I was about three years old, and we had a dog named Billy. He was a big black sheepdog. He had a sensitive spot on his back when he was run over. I remember playing with him, possibly jumping on his back when he bit me in the eye. I remember holding my eye while the warm blood gushed out screaming "Mom, Mom!" My mother was in the other room getting dressed when she heard my screams. I remember jumping in the back of our car with blood-covered hands. I blacked out after that until after the laser eye surgery when I woke up in a hospital bed. I had to wear an eye patch for weeks and for many years I had a scar on my left eye. Scars are interesting and I didn't know then, but scars represent trauma in a way.

It is easy to be abandoned when you are the last child. I remember a situation when I was at church and my family forgot to pick me up. It was a vague memory, and I don't blame my family for forgetting me. I was forgettable after my cute baby phase. I did not have sports like my brothers, and I was not a daddy's girl like my sister. I remember going to a lot of basketball and football games. We were a sports family.

My brothers and father were the most obsessed with sports. If they were not playing or practicing sports, they were watching sports. I did not like sports except basketball. I learned to dribble and shoot from my brothers. But besides basketball, I was not in the loop when it came to discussing sports. If anything, I started to avoid sports altogether and nobody in school knew who my brothers were unless they asked me.

I was the black sheep of my family. I liked to read and wanted to be a writer one day. My parents did not know what to do with me and it showed. They forgot me a lot because I was too good. I was the best child anyone could ask for because I was extremely quiet. I was quiet and reserved and you could hear a pin drop when I was around. I used to win at quiet games and teachers would love me. Teachers would move the kids who got into trouble next to me and hoped my goodness would rub off onto them. I realized I was good because I did not act like a regular child. My parents, from the beginning, did not have to worry about me.

It is easy to forget someone who does not seem to act out and when my siblings acted out, my parents came running with excuses and reasons. "Your siblings need help" my parents would reason when I pleaded to understand. "Your problems are not horrible enough" my parents would excuse the obsession with fixing my sibling's problems. I felt true loneliness as a child when my parents looked over me and it still lingers on me as an adult. I don't blame my parents or my siblings for forgetting me as a child. I did not act out or participate in sports. I was truly the black sheep.

CHAPTER 2: BODY IMAGE

I remember being average for a child until the summer before my second-grade year. I overindulged that summer. I was sedentary and the only thing I did all day was watch TV. I watched Nick at Nite late into the night. It is easy to overindulge when parents do not think there is any problem at all. I realized that besides sports, my family was consumed with watching TV. I had my favorite channels including Disney Channel and Nickelodeon. That summer I was able to watch TV for days without thinking of the consequences. I was only seven years old, and I had an addiction. Well, I had two addictions TV and food. I ate too much food. My stomach was always full, and I just kept eating thinking it would fill this emptiness or boredom I was feeling at the time.

Food was my enemy and those who brought up my weight were wrong. I knew I was fat, but I did not think about my body. I was only a child. I remember a time when my mom called my fat "baby fat." I honestly did not believe that I had that as a baby. I was an average human for six years of my life until something happened, and I became fat.

I could throw a pity party because I was a fat kid, but I am now a fat adult. There was one time in my life when I weighed 15 pounds less. I remember when others looked at me differently when I lost that fat. My appearance was different, but I still felt the same. The weight loss may have helped my body feel healthy but inwardly I felt extremely lonely and sad. Nothing I could do could change the fact I was forgettable.

Even though my parents decided not to see me. My siblings saw everything that was wrong with me. I didn't have baby fat. I was fat and I needed to do this or do that to be accepted by my peers. If I didn't meet my siblings' expectations, I was literally nothing to them. Ironically, I became successful and have risen far beyond the expectations my siblings had for me, but I am still fat.

I remember when I finally realized my body was changing. The bags of fat on my chest started to bounce up and down on a dirty school bus. I was in sixth grade and twelve years old. I held them down embarrassed, hoping nobody was looking at my chest. That was the first time I felt weird in my body. My sixth-grade year was the first time I felt true body shame. Before then I was just a fat kid. Now I was growing up in places and experiencing things I did not fully understand.

It felt weird getting my period for the first time. My parents, specifically my mother, did not really explain to me about my period. I remember being obsessed with understanding my body. I looked up periods online before I even experienced my first period. I was excited to get my period but since then realized how periods can be horrible. I remember not tracking my cycle and getting a shocking surprise every month. I did not get the sex talk and found out about sex online and by word of mouth. It was easy to be ashamed of being a woman when I felt uncomfortable in my body.

Even though puberty is normal, I felt uncomfortable in my own skin. It was easier being a fat kid than being a fat adolescent. I was bullied in high school and middle school because of my appearance. I was told I was fat and ugly. Honestly, I agree that I was fat, but I rather hide in embarrassment than be confronted that I was heavy. My brothers would talk about my weight all the time. It was too much of a focus for them and I realized that they were afraid of being fat. I felt like I was bullied by my brothers but then again, I was sensitive when it came to my body. I don't blame them now because they wanted me to be healthy. I get that I was not being healthy. I blame myself for being overweight and eating too much. I did not grow up with someone helping me balance my eating habits. I was not taught healthy eating habits and had an addiction to food.

CHAPTER 3: MENTAL HEALTH

My anxiety started when I was a child. I did not know what to call it. I just remember having an upset stomach every day. I know that being in pain every day did not help my anxiety. I felt anxious about everything. My anxiety really amplified in middle school. I remember having a really hard time sleeping at night. I was deathly afraid of spiders and when I thought a spider was in my room, I would stay up all night watching for the spider.

I had a lot of social anxiety and had a hard time making friends. It was easier being alone than trying to talk to other people. I hated calling people and felt anxious anytime I had a social gathering with other people besides family. I would say that my anxiety caused me not to take chances or try new things. It was easier to stay in my comfortable box than try and fail. I was afraid of failing and when I did fail, I felt like a complete failure to my parents.

My anxiety created my depression. My depression did not come into the picture until my sixth-grade year. I remember hating myself so much I was planning to commit suicide. I had a difficult time with my body and being forgotten by my family. I think these things with anxiety created an intense depression. I remember thinking that once my first nephew was born, I would die, eventually. It was difficult to keep going at that time.

It felt like I always had a dark cloud looming over me.

In high school, I wrote dark poetry and wrote in a blog to help me cope with these dark emotions. It helped somewhat but I still felt my depression and anxiety. I did not receive help for my depression and anxiety until college when I was encouraged to get therapy. It helped me cope with my depression, but it was not until I started taking antidepressants that I stopped having an upset stomach and my anxiety decreased significantly. Even though I have been able to cope with my anxiety and depression it still has been a lifelong struggle.

CHAPTER 4: FRIENDS AND LOVERS

I did not expect to be liked. I was a fat kid. I would not say I was exactly ugly, but I had a great personality, and I was funny. I was a funny fat kid. I loved elementary school, specifically fourth grade. I had the best teacher and I felt like I could have fun in that class. I had multiple crushes in this class, but I think the only boy I wanted attention from was my first crush. He was so sweet, and he loved to laugh with me. I loved it! I felt like he could accept me and that we could have fun together.

Instead of laughing with me my class laughed at me when I said that I liked a bunch of boys. It hurt and I realized I started to not trust people at all. I remember writing a note to another friend in the class about who I liked. She spread it throughout the class, and I was made fun of for liking boys. I thought it was normal in some way because I was fat, and I did not feel likable.

I did not realize that it was not okay to be laughed at because you like someone. I had a difficult time having crushes after that. It helped me to be shy because I did not have to face my future crushes. I was barely feeling infatuation and I was rejected. I did not want to feel rejected again, so I hid my emotions and secluded myself. When I had crushes in middle or high school,

I kept it hidden. It was easy to hide how I felt because I felt shame for feeling anything at all.

I thought my first crush liked me because, in high school, he asked me for my number. I think he may have been interested in me, but I was stuck on my own insecurities that were amplified by my class laughing at me while in fourth grade. Ironically, my first crush turned out to be gay and would not have ended up with me anyways. I think we all remember our first crush because it can feel like you are being crushed.

* * *

I did not experience a real relationship till I was nineteen years old. But before then I discovered that it was difficult to like anyone. I had crushes throughout middle and high school and all of them ended nowhere. It was easier to be distant than to be crushed again. In middle school, I liked a guy that was popular. He was liked by all the girls because he was sweet and kind. At church dances, he would dance with a lot of the girls. He was not a player but a nice guy. Most people liked to be around him. I think it was easier to not be noticed when a guy is flattered by so many others. I knew nothing was going to happen because of his popularity. I was the quiet fat girl.

In high school, I did not experience dances. I was never asked out on a date or asked out to prom. That part of my high school experience was nonexistent. I felt left out of this high school tradition. I think it felt worse because I felt like no boys would ask me out on a date. I think the lack of dates really hurt my self-esteem. It would be easy to say that it was just school dances and was considered not a big deal. It mattered to me because I was not seen by the boys at school.

I had a crush on a friend. I don't remember how it happened, but I had a friend group during my freshman year of high school. He was the only boy in this friend group. I did not feel as lonely that year of school. It was my sophomore year when this friend group split up into other groups and I felt lonely. I did not split up into one group because I made friends in separate groups. I bounced from one group to the next feeling like I had no home. I felt increasingly anxious knowing I had nowhere I belonged in high school. My guy friend turned out to be both distant and mean. He did not seem to have feelings for anything. I don't remember what attracted me to him besides his persona. He loved to play the piano and I enjoyed listening to him play. Besides his abilities, I don't remember anything good about him. I knew nothing would come of it because he did not like me.

I had a crush on a kid who debated. It was easy to like someone who was oblivious that girls liked him. I kept my distance, so I did not get hurt. He was too smart, and he did not notice I existed. It was not until I was in college that he paid attention to me. We both worked in the same job and ended up talking almost every day. We liked each other and went on a couple of dates till he realized we wanted different things in life and dumped me.

I then had a crush on a guy whom I could see a future with, but we met at different times in our life. He was two years younger than me, and I was about to graduate high school. I let my shyness be my crutch and had a hard time verbalizing anything around him. I dreamed of marrying him and he wanted the same things I did. I put him on a pedestal and did not see his weaknesses. He ended up marrying someone else around the time I married for the first time. He was the one who got away, and it still hurts to know I missed out on a great love.

* * *

I remember thinking I knew what love was until I met my first boyfriend. Love seemed to always be one-sided with me having crushes. I didn't experience someone loving me back until I met my first boyfriend at the tender age of 19 years old. I was in my second semester at college when I first talked to him. My best friend told me this guy from church wanted to date her, but she was not interested. I told her if she gave me his number, I would get him off her back. I did not think we would start flirting because I was on a mission to get him off my friend's back. I realized he was a sweet guy and that he lived in my hometown.

'When I visited home from school, we went on our first date. I don't remember it that clearly, but I remember seeing him for the first time. He was obese and had a nice smile and kind eyes. He liked to wear fedoras and he worked in the medical field. We became official after that first date, and we texted every day.

I remember always being extremely anxious because I had low self-esteem. I expected him to find someone else and dump me. I overthought everything in our relationship. When he said he loved me and that he wanted to marry me someday. It scared me. I was still a virgin and I never kissed anyone. This was my first real relationship, and I was beginning to understand how it felt to truly love someone for the first time.

My first boyfriend was also my first kiss. It was romantic as we had a picnic in the park. It was during a sunset, and we were talking about how I had not kissed anyone. He said he would go slow but when I turned my head, he kissed me passionately. He put his tongue down my throat and his kisses were wet. It felt extremely weird. He could not take his hands or lips off me after that. I remember being innocent even though I made out with my boyfriend a lot.

I remember when we first started really arguing. We argued about money and that he could not pay for dates all the time. We then argued about small things that I overthought constantly because of my anxiety. When it was time to go back to college, I think it was the nail in the coffin. Our relationship was over when I mentally pushed him away because of my low self-esteem, anxiety, and depression. The last straw was an argument we had that resulted in him saying he did not want to talk to me for a week. It was the worst week of my life. I cried every day, and my depression became increasingly worse. When the day came when he finally talked to me, he broke up with me over a text message.

The way he broke up with me still feels cruel to me. I experienced true heartbreak for the first time in my life and I was only 19 years old. The breakup caused a ripple effect where I did not care about having another relationship. If anything, I did not want to feel the pain I experienced after feeling the most passion and love I had in my life. I think I gave up.

After the breakup, I did give up on finding real love. I went after guys who did not have the same morals as I did. It was easy to find a guy who just wanted pleasure rather than an actual relationship. It was a dark time after my first boyfriend, and I experienced this disconnect with men. During this time, dating apps were widely known and it was easy to meet a man on the internet. I don't think I thought of internet safety when I started meeting up with random guys in person. I did not go past kissing and I am glad I didn't because all these guys ghosted me after we met in person.

Besides one guy who ended up being my second boyfriend. He was different and lacked the morals I had. I was pushed over the edge and felt complete shame. This guy seemed sweet and was an EMT. He was always on call for his job. He lived in this tiny one-room apartment, and he lived alone. His bed was in the middle of his apartment. I knew it felt wrong, but I went to his apartment by myself, and we made out a lot. So much for internet safety because I can see now how dumb I was. He could have been a maniac but honestly, my second boyfriend had secrets.

He dealt with depression and anxiety. When we text messaged or talked, he was always so depressed. He made my depression worse, and he told me multiple times that he was going to kill himself. It should have been a red flag for me to end the relationship right there, but I felt lonely, and we liked making out. When he said he was bisexual. I honestly was worried that he would have even more of an opportunity to find someone else. Then when he told me about his darkest secrets, he found me more attractive because I looked pregnant. But what really made me sick to my stomach was that he had sex with dogs. I think that was the worst thing about this guy.

Nobody knew that this guy had these secrets and they saw him as a nice guy I was dating. When I finally came to my senses, I was in Las Vegas visiting my brother. I saw a bunch of guys whom I could have dated, and I realized that I was settling for this guy that was not right for me. Weird how after all the weird and disturbing secrets, the nail in the coffin of this relationship was the potential I saw for my future. Ironically, I did exactly what my first boyfriend did to me. I broke this guy's heart over a text message. My romantic relationships seemed to get worse, and I wish I could say that my second boyfriend was the end of these disturbing relationships. It was not until the next relationship that I experienced abuse and trauma that seemed to haunt me for the rest of my life.

DURING

CHAPTER 5: UTAH TRIPS

I was growing up in a time when it was normal to meet up with people online. It is easier to talk to a screen than it is to talk to someone in person. I was not on a dating app when I met my ex-husband, I was on Facebook. It was specifically in a Facebook Latter-Day Saint group. I did not know then, but my ex-husband was looking for someone gullible. I had low self-esteem, and it was easy for me to let things slide even if they were against my values. He pretended to be in the church when he had been excommunicated. It is easy to see now that he was trying to find someone even it if was based on lies.

I was currently in college when I met my ex-husband. I was living with three other roommates, but I felt secluded. My roommates were independent and distant. Before I moved, I was living with five other roommates, and even though it started to get old with the drama. I missed that my roommates did not hide in their rooms all day or play video games all night. Even though I felt extremely lonely, I decided to stay at school in the summer months instead of going back home. I was almost done with college, and I just wanted to feel independent. I got a job during this time because I was taking a few classes. I remember not being able to pay for groceries and ending up starving myself. It was difficult being alone.

I remember that he commented on a post in the group, and I think we started talking from that point forward. He was in Utah, and I was in Idaho. I don't know what possessed me to go down to Utah to meet this guy besides the fact that I already have gone to see my ex-boyfriend by myself before and this seemed normal. I took the bus down to Utah by myself. I could not fathom doing this by myself now. I was stupid to think that this guy I was meeting up with was normal. We met at the Salt Lake airport, and we took the Trax (Utah train) everywhere even though he had no money. So, we were already breaking the law.

He had no car and I always thought it was weird that someone did not have a car. He told me he had a car wreck, and he was never able to get a car again. We walked everywhere and it was not fun. Sometimes he would have friends take us places but mostly we would use the Trax (Utah train) or walk places. He would always be in a hotel even though he did not have much money. It was either he was in a hotel, or he was in a home for drug addicts.

We were alone a lot and I believe he took advantage of that. He made me take showers with him even though it made me uncomfortable. He saw me bare naked before we were married. I was a virgin before I met him, and he seemed to push the boundaries I had when it came to sexual activity. I did not know much about sex because my parents never had a conversation about it with me. My high school did not provide me with much information except sexual diseases. Besides the fact that he pushed my boundaries, he was obsessed with virgins. It made sense because I was a virgin and, in the end, he did what he wanted with me.

CHAPTER 6: JULY 4, 2015

The 4th of July used to be my favorite holiday before my grandparents passed away, specifically my grandparents on my mother's side. I did not know my father's parents. My grandpa Clark passed away before I was born, and my grandma Clark only knew me as a child before she passed away. I remember the last time I saw my grandma Clark and it was on Halloween. She was watching an old person's TV and her home had a specific smell that sometimes when I go into an old building, I may encounter that exact smell.

My father always said I remind him of my grandma Clark but the fact that I don't remember her much says a whole lot about the time I did get to spend with her. I remember her giving me a China doll that I broke as a child. She used to collect dolls and figurines in villages. I received this small figurine house and an old book after she passed away.

My sister was able to spend the most time with my grandma Clark and to say that I am jealous of this comradery was an understatement. I wanted to know this mysterious figure that my father says I remind him of and being the last child did not do me any favors. I wish I knew my grandpa Clark, but my father does not speak much about his parents, and I find myself wondering what type of people they were in this world.

I knew my mother's parents well and it helped that they lived in the same town as me. It was usually the holidays that I would see my grandparents including the 4th of July, birthdays, Thanksgiving, and Christmas Eve. When my last living grandparent passed away, I honestly felt empty. I remember taking for granted the times I saw my grandparents and the 4th of July in 2015 was one of them.

I was the closest to my grandma Brandt, but I remember seeing both of my grandparents more often before my grandfather passed away. I was 12 years old, and I started walking down the street to see my grandparents from school. I picked apples with my grandpa Brandt, and I find myself wondering if those apple trees still exist today. My mom thought it was weird that I started to wander down the street to my grandparents' house instead of taking the bus home from school.

As an adult, I am glad I made those memories with my grandparents because that same year my grandfather fell and had a huge bruise on his face. My grandpa Brandt went downhill after that, and he passed peacefully in the nursing home. I remember the entire Brandt family singing to my grandpa and him being happy that everyone was around him before he went to heaven.

My grandma Brandt was still alive when I met him. She was living alone in that big house that was remolded years ago. She couldn't go upstairs anymore and just lived on the first floor. My grandma was obsessed with her mail and a family member had to help her with financial issues because she kept sending money to charities and getting scammed. My grandmother had a big heart and evil people used that against her. I remember how lonely my grandmother was that year. It was easy to see that not many people went and saw my grandmother. The family may call her and visit her occasionally, but she seemed lonely and depressed. I think this is why I feel guilty for not spending that time with her on the 4th of July. My grandmother would pass away the year after I married my second husband after having a stroke the day after Christmas. The last time I saw her we went to McDonald's and took her home from the hospital. The last words I said to her were "I love you."

It was easy to see that he was pushing me away from my family. I would not initially go away with a man to another state on the 4th of July. I would usually see fireworks and have a barbecue with my family. I was completely isolated on July 4th, 2015. We ended up walking up this mountain in Bountiful, Utah. We sat next to these nice homes and saw the fireworks go off around the entire Salt Lake Valley. I would say that it could have been an incredible experience, but I was with him.

CHAPTER 7: RED FLAGS

I was blind to love. My family told me he was not good for me, but I persisted. My dad thought he would not ever bring me back home after we were married. I can see others were afraid of him. I was afraid of his anger. His anger may have been innocent frustration, but it was borderline sadistic. We would walk and someone would look at him wrong and he would go off on this stranger. I am pretty sure I blacked out how he presented his anger to the world because it scared me so badly.

His anger seemed worse when he was sober. He softened a little bit when he started his drug of choice again. It was a cycle of him getting on and off substances that felt like a roller coaster. His moods seemed to change dramatically, and I dealt with the repercussions. He was sober when I met him and when we married, he found drugs again. He would get so angry he would break furniture in our tiny one-room apartment. He broke a broom and cut it in half with his bare hands. I passed this broken broom one day as I came up from doing laundry and it cut my foot open. He did not flinch and was so passive to my screams. I still have that scar on my foot that seems to always remind me that I was with him.

I wish I could remember all the things he did that were

warning signs. He was in jail for various things and his ex-wife had a restraining order on him. His ex-wife did not want him to see his twin boys. I can see the reasons why she did not want him in her life. He was a charmer, but he was psychologically, mentally, and emotionally abusive. I did not receive any physical abuse while with him, but I can see it eventually coming to that especially when it came to him threatening to physically harm me.

I blame myself for not seeing the warning signs that I can clearly see now. He was extremely controlling and wanted to isolate me from my family and friends. It was him against the world and I was on for the ride. He did not like cops or authority figures. When I called the police because he looked like he had a seizure he was furious with me. He did not want to go to jail and after they checked him out, he went to jail for the first time in our marriage.

He liked to blame others for his misdeeds. It was so and so's fault that he is abusive now. He was abused as a child, and he brought that up multiple times. He blamed me for calling the cops even though he was the one who had drug paraphernalia on him. It is easy to see from the outside perspective that the relationship was toxic, but I think it did not matter because I both loved and feared him.

CHAPTER 8: JUST MARRIED

I remember the day I got married for the first time. I went to the Goodwill store, and I picked out a maroon dress and a sweater that could tie up like a bow. He wore his Sunday best with a white shirt and black pants. We got married at a park in Utah. It was a beautiful day outside and it was a quick service.

Our church set the whole thing up for us and the bishop married us. The only family that showed up were my parents.

It was very short notice for them to come down to Utah. I remember my father being very nervous after the service. They drove us back to the hotel and my father asked me to come back with them. I was in love and nothing my dad would say would make me go back with him and my mother. I wish I did.

The first thing we did when we went to the hotel was to get ready for sex. I was nervous. I was a virgin and he wanted to claim his prize. I remember being anxious and excited. I didn't think he would be rough, and I didn't think he would ignore my screams. I said no and he kept going. I still have nightmares about it. He bore his weight on top of me, and he rammed into me. I was a prize he won. It was easy to think that our sex life was the easiest thing about our marriage. He would do his thing and then he would leave me lying there alone. I felt cheap every time. I could sense that he did not care if I was in pain. He did not show empathy toward me, and this was evident when he did not move when I tore my foot open with the broom he broke out of his rage.

The best thing that has happened to me the past couple days is hearing my husband say that everyday he falls in love with me even more. Your amazing ▮▮▮▮▮▮▮▮▮▮.

It's amazing waking up to someone who loves and cares about me. Who prays for me and reminds us to pray together. Who laughs and cries with me. Who everyday makes me want to be a better woman. It's a blessing to have ▮▮▮▮▮▮▮▮▮▮ in my life.

He brainwashed me into thinking he was a good man. I posted how much I loved him on Facebook and tried to lie to the world about our marriage. It was wonderful, I would write when behind closed doors I would fear for my life. I did not deserve him, I would say but behind closed doors, he would manipulate me and threaten suicide multiple times. It was easy to lie to the world because then I could believe it myself. His rages would blow over and he would love-bomb me and apologize. He tells me he will change but he continues this endless cycle of abuse.

CHAPTER 9: NEW YORK

It was not long after we were married that we moved across the country to the state of New York where he was from. The furthest I have traveled from Idaho before this was California, so this experience was new to me. We moved in with his mother and two siblings. He had a younger sister whom he adored and a teenage brother. They all lived in a suburb of New York in a house and in some ways, it felt like home. The neighborhood felt like I was back at home in Idaho with these cozy houses and friendly neighbors. In some ways, the neighbors in that New York suburb were friendlier than my hometown. They would host neighborhood parties where everyone in the neighborhood would bring food, and drink, and chill with each other.

When I got off that airplane for the first time, the humidity hit me in the face. It felt like I was sweating all the time. It was crazy. I felt cultural shock walking around the huge city with these enormous and gigantic skyscrapers. Besides this everything was green. When we saw trees or grass it was extremely green.

I was not used to green because in Idaho most of the time it was brown or dead. I went on the subway for the first time in my life and we took a bus to his mother's home. It felt surreal and sometimes I wonder if it was a dream. I always wanted to travel but never had the money to do so and I was swept into this amazing experience of seeing another world for the first time.

His mother was kind to me when we stayed with her. She drove us places and was helpful. When we first arrived, we lived in the basement, and we slept on a naked mattress. It did not last long though because he was able to manipulate his mother to have us sleep in a bedroom on the main floor. It was the only time in our relationship that I was okay that he manipulated the situation. He wanted the best for us, and he provided for it at the time. It took him probably less than a day before we had our own room in the house. I was grateful for that.

MORE THAN JUST OFFICE SUPPLIES.
Premier
Subway

Besides the living arrangements, I would say I was the loneliest I have ever been during this time. I stopped taking my antidepressants and I was heading into a severe depressive episode. I remember lying in bed staring into the distance and feeling emotionally numb. He seemed like he was in his element, and it was easier for him to get his drugs. He was different on his drugs, and I believe he seemed less angry and less abusive. He played his PC games and smoked his weed all day long. When neighbors or friends came over his mom, him, and his brother would do drugs and drink. I would be the only sober one besides his little sister.

It was isolating and I was very lonely. I did not have friends or family to talk to. He did not want me to talk to my family because he said they would say rude things about him. He wanted me all to himself. He knew that if I tried to talk to my family, they would say things because they were worried about me. Even though he asked me to do drugs with him, I never did. I think it was easy to say no because I already made the decision to stay sober. I remember seeing all these people act like idiots while drunk or on drugs and I just could not bring myself to want to participate. I am grateful I had one semester of college left because I had to come back to Idaho so that I could finish college.

CHAPTER 10: BACK TO SCHOOL

My father had to help us get plane tickets so that I could come back to school. It was difficult because it was the first time in my life that I asked for money. I was used to being independent and I did not want to become like my siblings who asked my parents for money all the time. It got to the point that my dad just expected every time my siblings would call, they needed help or money from him. I was becoming the person I did not want to become.

While at school we lived in married housing in a one-bedroom apartment. The only time I had time alone was when I was in the bathroom. It felt claustrophobic and I ended up taking a lot of baths to get away from him. He would explode where he would break furniture and our apartment seemed to always be messy with his drug paraphernalia everywhere. We did not have much of a kitchen, but I took a cooking class and started cooking for him. I tried to make this one-bedroom apartment home, but it was difficult. I asked him to go to couples counseling with me, but he only went one time, and the entire time he blamed me for everything.

* * *

My best friend had kittens that she and her aunt were giving away. We took two kittens and named them Simba and Moonlight. We were not supposed to have animals in the apartment, but they were a happy addition to the atmosphere. He seemed to take his anger out on the kittens. He would throw them around, specifically Moonlight. She did not recover from the abuse and

was distant in demeanor. Simba was still cuddly and loving even if he got abused. He would try to drown the cats and they would loudly whine. It pained me to listen to innocent animals getting hurt. I felt powerless because his rage scared me. I wanted to keep the kittens safe, but it was difficult. It was a huge red flag that he abused animals. I am angry that he was able to hurt them so much and was glad when they were not around him anymore.

* * *

I remember when he ran out of drugs, he needed money, so he sold my wedding ring which we were still paying on. It was a pretty ring that I picked out before we were married. I remember I was playing Mario Brothers on the Wii when a couple came by and paid for the ring in cash. I would say it was hard to give away something that he gave me. We were married and I loved him. But he did not care, and he sold it anyways

We went to Colorado to get his drugs. He had a friend in Colorado who had a job at a nice hotel. We took a nice, rented car and I remember driving for hours. We took turns driving the ten-plus hours to Colorado. I remember being proud of myself for driving on the freeway because before this I was extremely fearful of driving on the freeway. I think my confidence in my driving abilities increased which was the only positive thing that happened on that trip. He got his drugs, and we stayed in this nice hotel. We had a hot tub in the hotel room which was fancy. His friend hooked us up because he wanted drugs as well. I remember how weird the roads were in Colorado

When we got back to Idaho, he told me that he got this type of cannabis oil which was new. He was playing games on his computer when he started seizing. His body fell off the chair he was sitting in, and his body started to spasm. I was scared and the first thing I did was call the cops forgetting he had drug paraphernalia in the apartment. After the EMT checked him out he did not seem okay, but they took him to jail because of the drugs. I remember him being propped up on the bed and eventually getting back to reality. He was angry with me, and I could see it in his eyes. I messed up. The cops took him in handcuffs, and I was alone. I remember I took a bath after the incident and ended up crying for a long time. I told his family about the incident, and they did not believe that cannabis oil would cause seizures. It was weird that they did not believe something that I just witnessed. When he got out of jail, we had sex and of course, he left me alone afterwards. I felt alone like when he went to jail.

***

I remember during this time that he would threaten to commit suicide. I called the suicide hotline several times wondering what I should do. They were not helpful. They could not tell me how to deal with a manipulative person. He manipulated me into thinking he was the victim of everything. This is the second time I had to deal with a man who cried suicide. It was exhausting and I believe he easily manipulated me because I loved him

During this time, he was still talking to other women even though we had been married for a couple of months. He made me feel insecure because he talked badly about me to another woman. It felt weird having to continually stand up for myself to my husband. It was easy for him to blame me for things. I wish I could say that his mind games did not mess with my head, but they did. I remember reading his text messages on his phone and thinking how awful it is that he does not even like me

CHAPTER 11: DECEMBER 2015

I remember skipping classes and not feeling in the right headspace to be a student. I was ready to graduate and felt like I was skimming by on bad grades. It was a miracle I passed any classes at this time. I was ready to be done with school because I felt like I continually failed myself as a student. I had a horrible GPA after I graduated college. I remember waiting to talk to the professor about my internship class. It seemed like everyone else passed the class. I walked in and had the news I was not expecting which was that I either must retake the course or graduate. I decided it would be best to graduate

I think my failure was an accumulation of things including my mental health. I was struggling with my anxiety and depression. My anxiety made it difficult to talk in front of large groups even though it was a subject I loved which was art. I felt uncomfortable being a teacher. I felt deeply depressed, and it was difficult not to feel numb. People would notice that I was not mentally present when I had to be the teacher. I was barely holding on to the motivation to finish college. Besides this, the abuse I received at home was so severe I felt alone. I remember the loud bangs and cat screams that always came from my tiny one-room apartment. I was embarrassed because our neighbors could hear the abuse through these thin walls. I don't think they called on us because I never had anyone come to the door to check on us if we were okay. I did not have anyone check on me to see if I was okay. I was not okay.

* * *

I graduated on December 5, 2015, with a bachelor's degree in general studies. I remember my parents came to see me walk and that he sat next to them. The graduation program was very long, and he did not pay attention to anything. My parents told me he was so caught up in his phone he did not look up once. I remember getting lost after the service and having a difficult time finding my parents and him. We ended up taking awful photos in the gym because it was too dark outside to take nice ones. My dad always says that it is crazy that I graduated in the first place. He was right

After I graduated, we did not end up staying at the college. We went to my parent's house for Christmas and the holidays. We took our two cats and ended up staying in my brother's old room. We had a normal Christmas and I ended up buying him a nice knife from Amazon. I would not expect him to hurt others with it. Besides the fact he was snorting his ADHD medication, he seemed normal. It ended up being the catalyst for the scariest night and day of my life

CHAPTER 12: THE LAST NIGHT

It seemed like a normal night I was watching TV and we had sex. Now that I think about it having sex at my parent's house was weird. I remember he snorted his ADHD medication and seemed off. I became extremely scared of him after his behavior became increasingly worse. He put his arm around me and told me he was going to strangle me. He laughed at my fear and said it was a joke. It felt real to me. I prayed that I would make it till the next day. I think that threat was the end for me. I think I woke up to his abuse. It was weird feeling like I was not blind to love anymore

I did not want to sleep that night. I did not want to know if he was going to do something to me. I felt like I was in trouble and that I was in an empty dark room trying to scream for help, but nobody heard me. I was extremely alone that night even though my parents were in the other room probably sleeping. I think I mentally blacked out his weird and scary behaviors. I remember thinking that if I did not get out of this relationship now, he would kill me. I would be one of those statistics of those women who have been brutally murdered by their spouses. The Lord heard my prayers that night because I woke up the next morning

CHAPTER 13: THE LAST DAY

I remember waking up in fear. He brought me breakfast and I felt like I had to act fast. I told my mom what he did the night before. He told my mom that I was the crazy one. He gaslighted me and tried to make me question everything. I went into the other room and called the police. It was the first time in months I felt powerful

When the cops came, I told them I could not be there anymore. They took me away from my parent's house while he stayed there. They took me to my sister's house which was down the street from my parents' house. While at my sister's house, she gave me anxiety medication that made me loopy. She saw how scared and anxious I was and thought it would help. I don't remember the reason why we went back to my parent's house. He was trying to get his stuff to leave when my brother showed up. They started to fight and began rolling around in my parent's living room

I remember my sister telling me to get outside the house and the police were called again. He had the knife I gave him for Christmas, and he threw it at my brother. I was not there because I felt loopy from the anxiety medication. I felt a rush of adrenaline that also did not help either. He was arrested and I wish that was the last time I saw him, but it was not. The last time I saw him he was in an orange jumpsuit, handcuffed, waiting for his conviction. He was in jail for six months and I served him divorce papers while he was in jail. I finally received my divorce papers on my birthday February 28, 2016

AFTER

CHAPTER 14: THE NEXT CHAPTER

L ooking back, it is difficult to comprehend that I could have been homeless. I remember when I was a teenager, joking that I may be homeless one day. Life felt real when I realized I could have ended up on the streets. My parents would not let that happen and I ended up living with my parents for a year. My mom was grateful that I was home because she seemed lonely when my dad went to work. I enjoyed the time I had with my parents, but I felt like a failure as an adult. Even though my ex-husband's choices were not my fault. I still felt guilty

The day after he was taken to jail, I began looking for a graduate program. He told me I should not look for more schooling and I felt I needed to keep going with my education. Graduate school was very expensive, and I ended up taking one course at a time until I finished with a 3.9 GPA after about seven years of school. I finished the year I turned 29 which meant I went to school my entire 20's.

I think I realize now, I put forth more effort in my education because my relationship with my ex-husband did not work out. I have done that a lot with previous relationship failures where I found a niche to help me keep occupied and help me grieve a relationship. I had to do something regarding my financial stability. I took a job that had fewer hours and less pay even though I deserved more. I remember taking jobs that I knew would not fulfill my needs or wants and feeling guilty for quitting them years or months later

Even though I am now graduated with a graduate degree, I feel like I am still not happy. It has been an uphold battle of working for a job that does not provide true happiness but only provides financial obligation. I find myself wanting more out of life

CHAPTER 15: DATING AGAIN

After my ex-husband, I was left scarred when it came to dating. I already had a difficult time with my self-esteem and body image, but it was amplified during my relationship with my ex-husband. It was difficult to trust my judgment and I did not trust men besides my father. I was drenched in guilt and shame from being in an abusive relationship.

I had to put out a restraining order on my ex-husband, so I felt safe. Ironically, I never felt safe especially when he was in the jail in the town I was living in at the time. I had these irrational fears that he was eventually going to come for me. I blocked him and his family on Facebook. I made it so nobody could see my location and had to make my information private. I had to make myself feel somewhat safe, but it did not work. I still had nightmares of the abuse.

At church I was going to the congregation my parents went to. I felt out of place and lonely. After a couple of weeks or months, I went to a single adult congregation. After months of being married, it was weird going to a singles ward. I felt extremely isolated and did not know how I was going to cope.

It seemed the only thing that they talked about was marriage. They wanted us to be married and to seek a companion. I did not see myself finding anyone again. Besides those nights when I felt extremely lonely, I could not fathom putting myself into the dating pool again.

Even though I knew single people, I did not date. It was difficult because there was not a lot of dating at church. If anything, people were more likely to online date than date those people they find at church. I went on dating apps again thinking it would be fun to go on dates again. I did not think I would find anything serious or that I would find another man to marry. I was about to quit dating altogether when a guy messaged me.

He was not perfect, but he seemed to have the same morals as I did. He did not want to only talk to me, he wanted to date me in person. We messaged each other then we talked to each other then he came and picked me up for a weekend date. I remember he was holding a stuffed bear and flowers. He picked me up in this beat-up car and he was not what I imagined. He was more attractive than his photos on the internet. He drove me across the state to meet his mother and his friends. On the way there he kissed me for the first time. He accidentally hit me with his back car door, and he took my face in is hands and kissed me lightly on the lips. Instead of extreme passion, he exhibited kindness. We both laughed at the kiss and kept going on our journey to his hometown

We went to a corn maze with his friends and walked through the maze together. We went to a state football game with his younger brother while it poured rain. We went to the temple which is a sacred place in our religion. We sat across from each other from an alter and did sealings of family members

and spouses. We believe in an eternal family, and we helped those families who passed away receive those blessings that day.

When I looked across that altar and looked into his blue eyes, it scared me because it felt right. I was scared he was going to hurt me like my ex-husband, but I realized during our entire relationship he was willing to sacrifice everything to be with me

After our first date, he came and visited a lot. He would continually surprise me and still does. He moved closer to my parent's house and then he asked me to marry him. Even though our engagement was not picture-perfect, I realized it did not matter in the end. Our wedding day was the happiest day of my life. Even though he did not completely cure me of my past trauma he still tries to understand it

CHAPTER 16: FAITH

My faith has been a huge part of who I am ever since I can remember. As a child, my parents would take me to church every week. I am a member of the Church of Jesus Christ of Latter-Day Saints formerly known as Mormons. My faith has been the driving force behind my actions

I was baptized when I was eight years old and received the Holy Ghost. The Holy Ghost is considered a friend who provides comfort and warnings. I remember times when I would receive these promptings from the Holy Ghost, and I would be able to find my lost glasses or receive comfort when I felt anxious.

When I grew up, I went to the temple to do work for my ancestors. I would get baptized and receive the Holy Ghost for those who passed on in the temple. They cannot do it because they do not have a body but by going to the temple, I can take an ancestor's place to help forward the work. When I was married to my ex-husband, I took out my endowments which were promises I would make to the Lord.

I find myself wondering how I could have taken out my endowments while being married to a man who had no morals. My ex-husband was excommunicated from the church. He took the missionary lessons and was baptized but it was through his actions that he was excommunicated. It was through my religion that he tricked me. It was a miracle I was able to take out my endowments, and the Lord knew I needed strength at the time. Looking back, I went to the temple more often doing the services for the dead. I felt strengthened every time I went to the temple.

Before my ex-husband went to jail providing a catalyst for our divorce, I was spiritually further away from God. I went to church every week for most of my life but during this time, I stopped going to church altogether. I felt isolated without that comfort I received from going to church. It was easy to push God away instead of realizing how much I needed him at the time. While being around drugs and abuse, I missed feeling God's love. I was able to go back to church and be able to feel God's love again after my ex-husband left for jail. It was through Christ's atonement I was able to deal with the abuse. He continues to strengthen me to this day.

CHAPTER 17: EPILOGUE

After I was married to my current husband, my ex-husband still tried to contact me through Facebook. He made another account just to contact me. I had to block that account as well. My restraining order was up after a year which was concerning. I tried to get a lifetime restraining order, but I did not go to court. It was honestly too much for me to process and I decided that my mental health was more important than facing him again.

He was done with his sentence after six months in jail. Instead of going back to New York, he decided to move only 30 minutes away from my parent's house. After a while, I stopped thinking about him or the abuse. It was not until a girlfriend of his contacted me and asked me about him that I had to revisit the worst time of my life. I told her the truth about him. It was difficult to rehash things I did not want to remember but I did hope she would leave him. She did leave him, and I did not hear from her again until 2020. He went back to New York by then, probably living with family.

The year 2020 was one of the worst years for a lot of people because of the shutdowns and Covid. When she contacted me, I did not expect her to say that he passed away. He was in his early thirties when he died. I was too curious to look up what happened to him. I tried to get some type of closure from the abuse. He was run over by a car, and I was not surprised. I was not shocked that there was a short article about his death. It was all surreal and I could not cope with the idea my abuser was gone. It was weird.

Even though I was married again, and it has been three years, it felt odd knowing I did not have to worry about my abuser ever again. He would never again try to catch me in my DMs on Facebook, make new profiles to contact me, or try to persuade me to get back with him. He was completely gone, and I was an empty shell of myself. I realized he still had me even though he was gone. His abuse haunts my nightmares and I find myself having a difficult time trusting others.

Fast forward to 2023 and it has been three years since I found out about his death. I wonder why the abuse I suffered still comes up in my daily life. I can see an abusive relationship a mile away and it is still triggering for me. Even if the abusive relationship has nothing to do with me, I find myself wanting to fix the broken. I realize he did break me in ways I cannot truly express. One day in church, I realized I needed to write my story. I decided it was the time to express those thoughts and feelings that had been weighing me down for years. I am grateful for this opportunity to show others you can get out of an abusive relationship. I was a victim of abuse and now I am a survivor. You can be a survivor too

About the Author

Maye Clark,30, was born in a small town in Idaho. She is the last of five children and has the best parents in the world. She has been married to her wonderful husband for 6 years and has a silly dog named Lady who keeps her on her toes. She has recently found her love of writing again and loves to create art in her free time